BASEBALL BAT

written by
H. I. Peeples

illustrated by
Chris Reed

A CALICO BOOK
Published by Contemporary Books, Inc.
CHICAGO · NEW YORK

A Calico Book
Published by Contemporary Books, Inc.
180 North Michigan Avenue, Chicago, Illinois 60601
Copyright © 1988 by The Kipling Press
Text Copyright © 1988 by Robert Cwiklik & Russell Shorto
Illustrations Copyright © 1988 by Chris Reed
All Rights Reserved.

Art Direction by Tilman Reitzle
Library of Congress Catalog Card Number: 88-19356
International Standard Book Number: 0-8092-4468-3
Manufactured in the United States of America

Published simultaneously in Canada by Beaverbooks, Ltd.
195 Allstate Parkway, Valleywood Business Park
Markham, Ontario L3R 4T8 Canada

Have you ever wondered where baseball bats come from? Do they fly in from the moon? Are they dug out of the earth like diamonds? Of course not! Baseball bats come from trees, from living things. They begin life deep in the forest, as tiny seeds that sprout stems and leaves, that drink rainwater and stretch to catch the warm sunlight.

Not all kinds of seedlings will grow into "bat trees." Ash trees are the best because ash wood is hard and firm, and also lightweight. As the seasons pass, the ash saplings stretch and grow. When the tree is about fifty years old, it is hard, tall, and mature. It is perfect for making bats.

A forester walks among the tall trees and chooses the best ones to be cut down. He taps the trunk. He measures it. He feels its strength and gazes high up to its top branches. Satisfied, he marks the trunk with paint. The mark tells the cutter that this is a perfect bat tree.

5

BZZZZZZZZ!!!
The cutter then goes to work. His saw bites into the base of the trunk and cuts a wedge on one side, then on the other. There is a loud groaning sound as the tree slowly tilts to one side. Then, with a sudden rush, it comes crashing to the ground. BOOOOM! The forest floor shakes from the force.

6

The cutter strips off all the branches, then saws the tall trunks into shorter sections. These are loaded onto the back of a truck with an enormous, clawlike machine. When the men have loaded dozens of logs onto the truck, the truck rumbles heavily off toward the lumber mill.

At the mill the logs roll past an important man who checks to make sure all the logs are of top quality. If a log has knots in it, or if it is warped, then he shakes his head. Only the straightest and smoothest logs pass his test, and these are then cut into bat-sized lengths.

8

The shortened logs are then split length-wise into six pieces. The pieces are fitted into a long cutting machine called a lathe. They spin around and around and the lathe shaves them into a rough round shape. These rounded forms are called billets.

9

These billets are still freshly cut wood, so they have a lot of water in them. Before they can be made into bats they have to dry out. The billets are stacked in the lumber yard under the sun to dry.

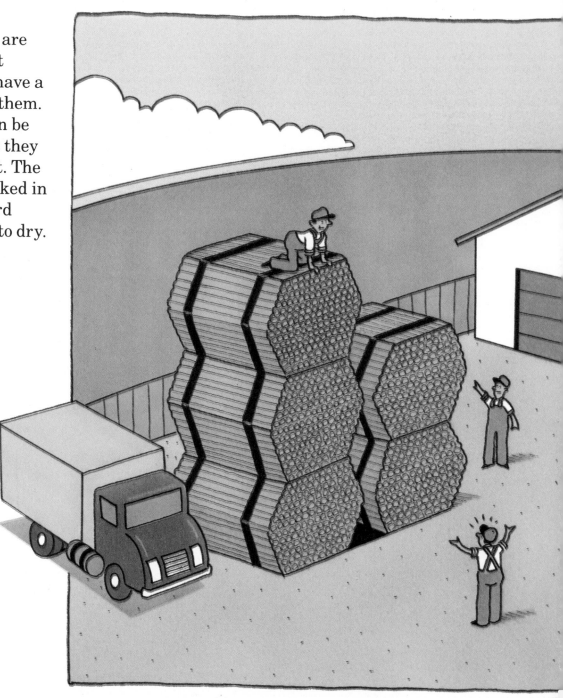

This can take a very long time — maybe as long as two years. It all depends on the weather conditions and how wet the wood is. The billets are not forgotten. Someone checks them regularly, and when he decides they are nice and dry he sends them into the mill.

Another sharp-eyed checker comes around and examines the billets carefully. He also weighs them to see if they have lost all their water. He is sure to spot some losers that aren't good enough to be made into bats. These are tossed into a heap.

The billets that have survived these tests are put onto another lathe. The lathe starts turning and chips fly. Suddenly the billet begins to look like a baseball bat.

13

Most billets spin around on a lathe where a machine does all the work. They are spun into regular bat shapes: tapered on the grip end where the handle is, and fatter at the other end, with a rounded top. The size ranges from about thirty inches to thirty-eight inches long.

But some of the billets are not finished by machines. These are the billets with the highest quality wood and the straightest grain. These are very skillfully finished by hand and will be used by professional baseball players. A master bat carver can make a bat just the way a pro wants it. Most pros are very picky.

15

Next, the bats are branded with the seal of the company, stained to give them a richer color, and finally given a smooth coat of varnish to protect the finish.

Dozen upon dozen, the brand new bats are stacked into boxes, ready to be sent to the stores. Did you know that over a million wooden baseball bats are made every year? A single bat may last you a long time, but the average professional uses seventy-two bats a season!

Orders come into the factory from all over the country. Boxes of bats are loaded on trucks and delivered to sporting goods stores, department stores, and toy stores.

Inside the store they are unpacked and stacked on display beside the baseball gloves, balls, caps, uniforms, and catcher's equipment. Customers like you and me walk in, pick up several bats, and choose one that feels just right.

19

It took fifty years for the tree to grow, and lots of work for the factory to cut it and shape it into bats and ship the bats to stores. And now, at last, comes the fun part: you get to PLAY BALL!

The pros may be able to hit the ball harder, but their bats come from the same place yours do. Practice makes the difference!

21

So now everytime you crack a double or pound a home run, you'll know all about how your good old bat got there. Unless, of course, it's an aluminum bat. But that, my friend, is another story.

ABOUT
THE
ARTIST

Chris Reed is an
illustrator living and
working in New York
City. He graduated
in 1983 from the
School of Visual Arts
and is mostly
involved with
magazine editorial
work. This is the
second book that he
has illustrated.
By the way, Chris is
an avid fan of the
Detroit Tigers and
loves to play baseball!